2017
WORLD CHAMPIONS
2019
2022
Lincoln Financial Field
4:15
PHILADELPHIA EAGLES
FLY EAGLES
EAGLES
BELIEVE
KELCE
62
BLANKENSHIP
32
33

PHILADELPHIA EAGLES – A PRIVATE COLLECTION

BRAZIL to BROAD ST

SKYBOX PRESS

THE EAGLES PREPARE TO ENTER THE INTENSE ENVIRONMENT AT ARENA CORINTHIANS IN SÃO PAULO, BRAZIL TO OPEN THE 2024 REGULAR SEASON

GRAHAM
57
STEEN

FOREWORD

BY JEFFREY LURIE

The 2024 Philadelphia Eagles season was truly an incredible performance by our entire organization from the time we began building our roster in the spring to the way we performed during training camp and the preseason leading into a remarkable regular season that began in Brazil. Winning three postseason games at Lincoln Financial Field in front of the best fans in the world and then playing the kind of start-to-finish game in New Orleans to win Super Bowl LIX demonstrated the power of blending our incredibly talented, humble, and selfless roster of players assembled by Executive Vice President/General Manager Howie Roseman and his staff, with a coaching staff led by Head Coach Nick Sirianni that maximized each and every player's skills.

Defeating the Kansas City Chiefs, 40-22, on February 9, 2025 served as a microcosm of one of the greatest football teams the NFL has seen in many seasons. Our defense, the top-ranked unit in the regular season, dominated the line of scrimmage and took the football away. Our offense made big play after big play and answered everything thrown at them. Our special teams won battles, both in the kicking and return games.

After that, it was a celebration unlike anything we have ever had in the City of Philadelphia, and sharing it with our global fanbase was what made it so special. The joy was palpable.

One of the themes of the 2024 Philadelphia Eagles season was, "You cannot be great without the greatness of others." This football team and organization believed that, lived that, and in the end, celebrated that with a second Lombardi Trophy and a World Championship celebration that we will all cherish forever!

CHAIRMAN AND CHIEF EXECUTIVE OFFICER JEFFREY LURIE CELEBRATES WITH THE VINCE LOMBARDI TROPHY ON THE SUPER BOWL PARADE ROUTE ON FEBRUARY 14, 2025

C
55

THE FIRST OFFICIAL MEETING BETWEEN HEAD COACH NICK SIRIANNI AND SAQUON BARKLEY IN COACH'S OFFICE SHORTLY AFTER SAQUON SIGNED HIS CONTRACT

NICK
SIRIANNI
EVERYDAY
IN
EVERYWAY
I AM
GETTING

EAGLES
C
2

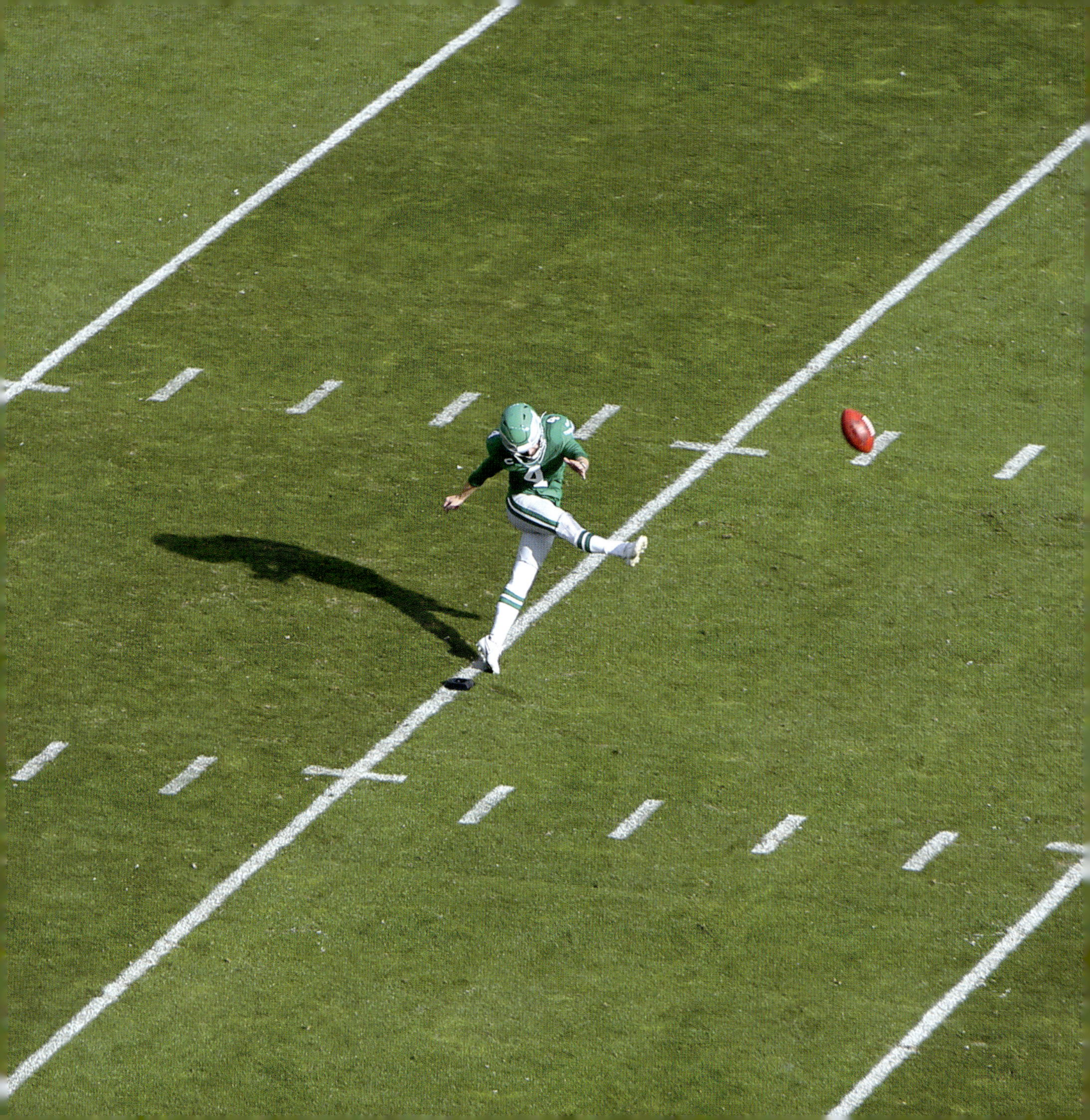

GRAHAM
55

EAGLES

34 - 29 (W)

THE SCENE AT ARENA CORINTHIANS IN BRAZIL
AS THE EAGLES AND GREEN BAY PACKERS PLAY
IN THE FIRST-EVER NFL GAME IN SOUTH AMERICA

0 TOL 3
0 TOL 3
0:49
QUARTER 1
DOWN
TO GO
BALL ON
VISA
EAGLES
55
68
2

EAGLE
SMIT

PACKERS
EAGLES

EAGLES
65
EAGLES
77
EAGLES
51

DJ
113
65
ELLISS
55
CARTER
0

88

15 - 12 (W)

vs. SAINTS

WK 03

EAGLES
88

"UNHOOK THE TRAILER, GODDAMNIT, UNHOOK!"
— JORDAN MAILATA

Microsoft
Surface
Microsoft
Surface
EAGLES
26

VIP

GRAHAM
55

S YOUR CHOICE
RAYMOND JAMES STADIUM
CRUCIAL
CATCH
INTERCEPT CANCER
IT'S YOUR CHOICE
Ford
FIFTH THIRD
AdventHealth
34
57

HURTS
1
NFL

Your tomorrow. Our priority.
Lincoln Financial
Lincoln Financial Field
American
TickPick
90
55
98

SWEAT
19
3

A GAME BALL FOR BRANDON GRAHAM IN HIS 15TH AND FINAL SEASON WITH THE EAGLES

CRUCIAL CATCH

28 - 3 (W)

vs. GIANTS

WK 07

EAGLES
11

74
26
EAGLES
26

O FIELD

EAGLES

EAGLES
NFL

GRAHAM
55
BAUN
53
HUFF
0

22

DOTSON
16
65

SMITH
6

"WE'RE EXECUTING AT A HIGH LEVEL RIGHT NOW."
– DeVONTA SMITH

28 - 23 (W)

vs. JAGUARS

WK 09

55
74

RUSHING - MATTISON: 8 ATT,35 YDS,0 TDS
BECTON SR
77
FLY EAGLES FLY

Lite
IT'S Miller TIME
25
SMITH
6

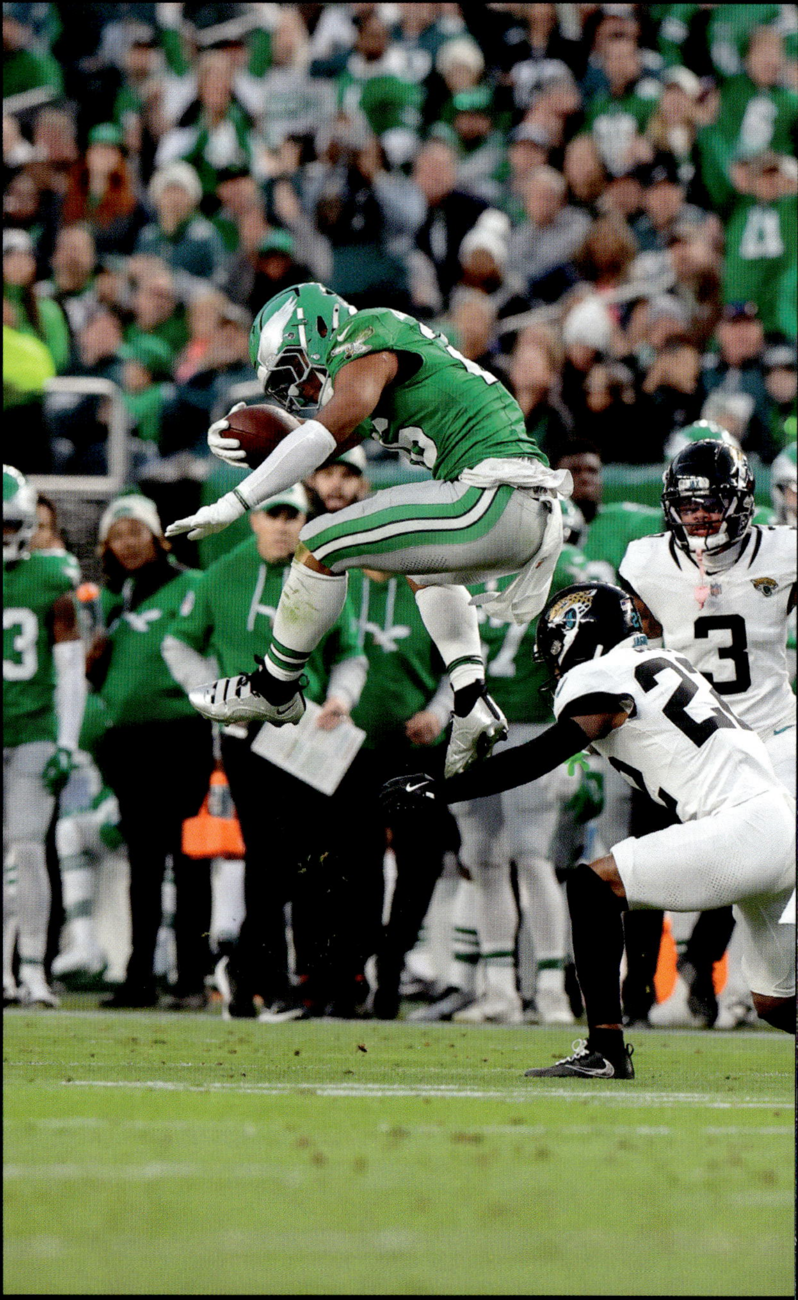

THE ICONIC LEAP AGAINST JACKSONVILLE, DESCRIBED BY SAQUON BARKLEY:

19
55
32
53
33
92
PHI

34 - **6** (W)

vs. COWBOYS

WK 10

SALUTE
TO SERVICE
EAGLES
NFL
NFL
NIKE

EAGLES
704

26

26 - **18** (W)

vs. COMMANDERS

WK 11

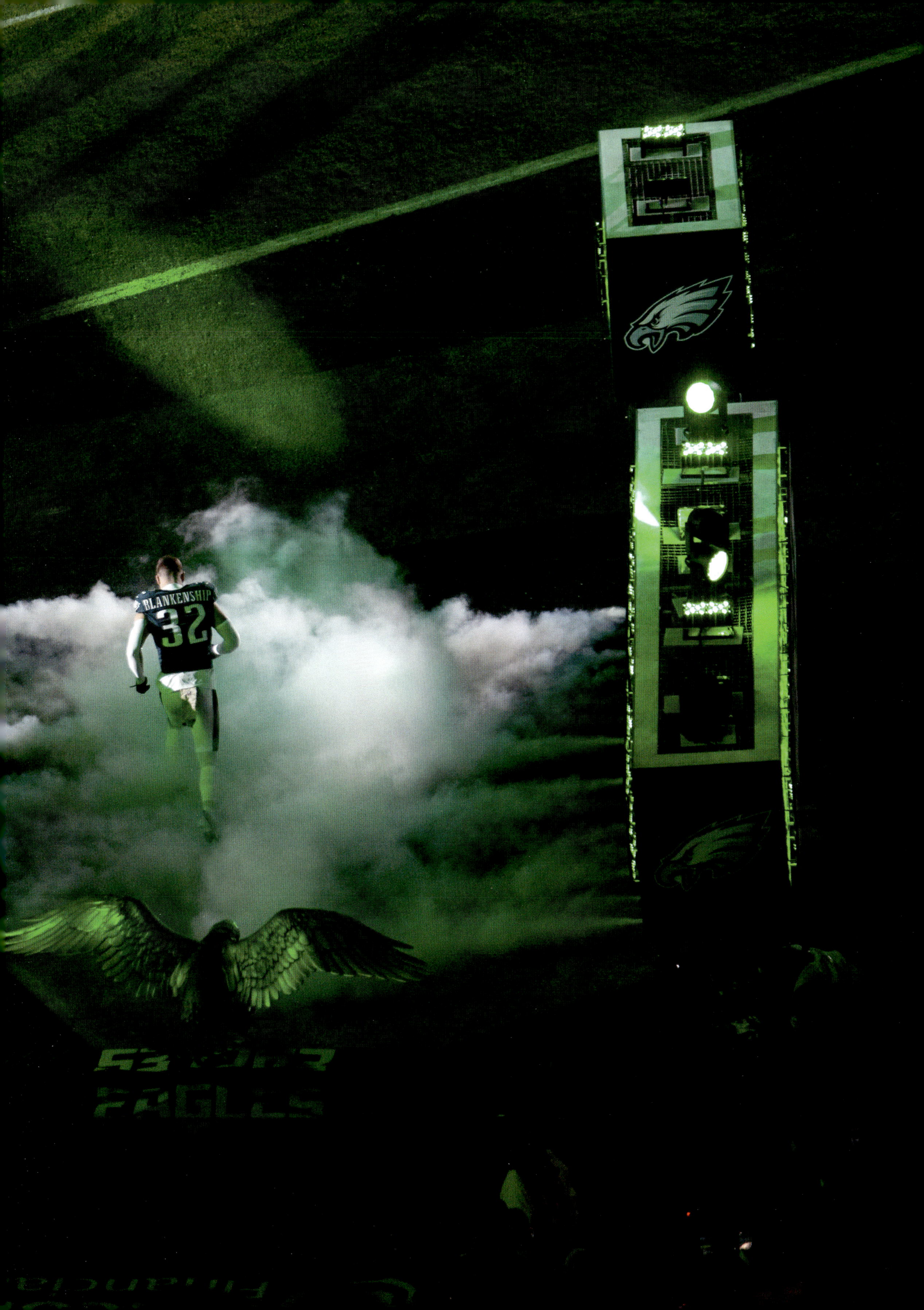
BLANKENSHIP
32

A.J. BROWN PRESENTS DeVONTA SMITH WITH A CAKE
ON HIS 26TH BIRTHDAY AS THE EAGLES EXTEND THEIR
NFC EAST DIVISION LEAD TO TWO GAMES

EAGLES

26

"I DIDN'T KNOW I WOULD HAVE THIS MUCH SUCCESS, BUT I'M THANKFUL TO BE HERE." — SAQUON BARKLEY

EAGLES
55
50

BROWN
11
HURTS
1
69
51

24 - 19 (W)

vs. RAVENS

WK 13

EAGLES
51
RAVENS
WASHINGTON
29

“THAT WAS OUR MESSAGE GOING IN — THAT THEY HAD TO MATCH OUR PHYSICALITY.” — COACH SIRIANNI

36
DEJEAN
33
22

8
93

GOEDERT
88
STEPHENS
21

EAGLES
23
EAGLES
34
EAGLES
27
EAGLES
29

22 - 16 (W)

VS. PANTHERS

WK 14

EAGLES

30

EAGLES
11

Jefferson
Health
KANGOL
Jefferson
Lincoln
Financial
Field
NFL
NFLN

"SO THAT'S WHAT Y'ALL WANTED TO SEE, HUH?"
— JALEN HURTS

73
22
Steelers
17
EAGLES

EAGLES
34

EAGLES
58

33 - 36 (L)

vs. COMMANDERS

WK 16

EAGLES
90
76

EAGLES

EAGLES
3
EAGLES
2

DAVIS
90
ELLIOTT

GO BIRDS
TURNOVERS

"ALL I WANTED TO ACCOMPLISH TODAY WAS TO GET THE WIN. FOR THE TEAM. FOR THE CITY." — KENNY PICKETT

EAGLES

SAQUON BARKLEY BURSTS OVER THE LEFT SIDE IN THE WIN
OVER DALLAS FOR A 23-YARD GAIN AND PASSES THE
2,000-YARD RUSHING MARK IN THE REGULAR SEASON

54
EAGLES
63

16
EAGLES
16

"I'LL BE READY WHETHER I'M THE NUMBER ONE [OPTION], THE TWO, THE THREE, THE SIXTH. WHATEVER IT IS." — TANNER MCKEE

NFL
EAGLES
21

26
90
NFL

NFL
EAGLES

NFL
WILD CARD

THE EAGLES DEFENSE LIMITS GREEN BAY TO 107 RUSHING YARDS AND FORCES THREE INTERCEPTIONS, EN ROUTE TO A WILD CARD WIN AT HOME

PACKERS
25
90

"I SLOWED DOWN SO HE COULD COME AND GET SOME."
— DALLAS GOEDERT

88
EAGLES

14
25

LET'S
HUNT

DOTSON
83

28 - 22 (W)

VS. RAMS

WK 20

ISAIAH RODGERS RETURNS A FUMBLE 40 YARDS
DOWN THE SIDELINE TO SET UP AN EAGLES' SCORE IN A
NFC DIVISIONAL WIN OVER THE LOS ANGELES RAMS

ROZE
EAGLES

EAGLES

EAGLES
11
56

EAGLES
26

"MY FAVORITE TOUCHDOWN SO FAR OF MY FOOTBALL CAREER SINCE I WAS A LITTLE KID." – SAQUON BARKLEY

SAQUON BARKLEY SCORES ON A 78-YARD RUN, PART OF A 205-YARD, TWO-TOUCHDOWN DAY THAT HELPS LIFT THE EAGLES PAST THE LOS ANGELES RAMS AND INTO THE NFC CHAMPIONSHIP GAME

Lincoln Financial Field

98

EAGLES

EAGLES

OJOMO

CHAMPIONSHIP

IN A TOTALLY DOMINANT PERFORMANCE, THE DEFENSE SHUTS DOWN WASHINGTON AS THE EAGLES GO ON TO WIN THE NFC CHAMPIONSHIP GAME

EAGLES

SMITH JR

EKELER
54

26
01
95

4
U
89

EAGLES
58

NATIONAL FOOTBALL CONFERENCE
CHAMPIONS

WREXHAM
WALES

40 - 22 (W)

DeVONTA SMITH HAULS IN A 46-YARD PASS FROM JALEN HURTS FOR THE TOUCHDOWN AND A 34-0 LEAD IN SUPER BOWL LIX

vs. CHIEFS

WK 22

SUPER BOWL

Champions

15
33

CHAMP

OAKLEY
SUPER BOWL
CHAMPIONS
SUPER BOWL
CHAMPIONS
PHILADELPHIA EAGLES
49

SUPER BOWL LIX
CHAMPIONS

SUPER BOWL
CHAMPIONS
LIX
PHILADELPHIA EAGLES

"THIS IS THE ULTIMATE TEAM GAME. YOU CAN'T BE GREAT WITHOUT THE GREATNESS OF OTHERS."
— COACH SIRIANNI

-14-25

SUPER BOWL PARADE

S · BROAD · ST
NO
TURN
ON RED

PHILLY'S OWN GILLIE DA KING LEADS THE WAY OUT OF LINCOLN FINANCIAL FIELD AS THE SUPER BOWL PARADE GETS STARTED!

SUPER
BOWL LIX

LIX

NFL
SUPER BOWL LIX
26
EAGLES
LOVE, HURTS.

THANK
YOU
FANS

CHAIRMAN AND CHIEF EXECUTIVE OFFICER JEFFREY LURIE SHOWS OFF THE VINCE LOMBARDI TROPHY TO THE CHEERING FANS OF PHILADELPHIA AT CITY HALL AMID CONFETTI, TEARS, AND LOVE

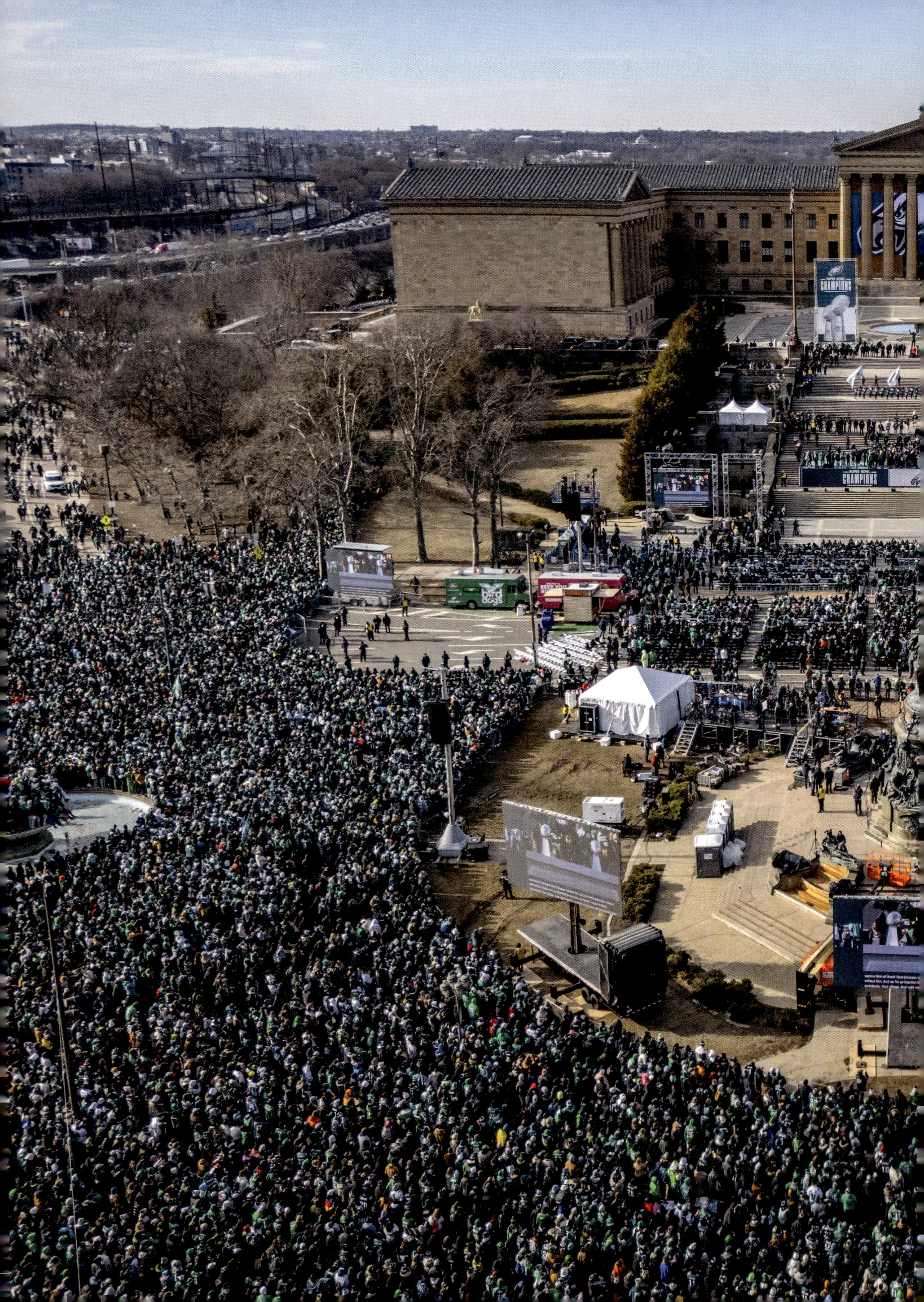
SUPER BOWL
CHAMPIONS
SUPER BOWL
CHAMPIONS
bird dogs
DUNKIN

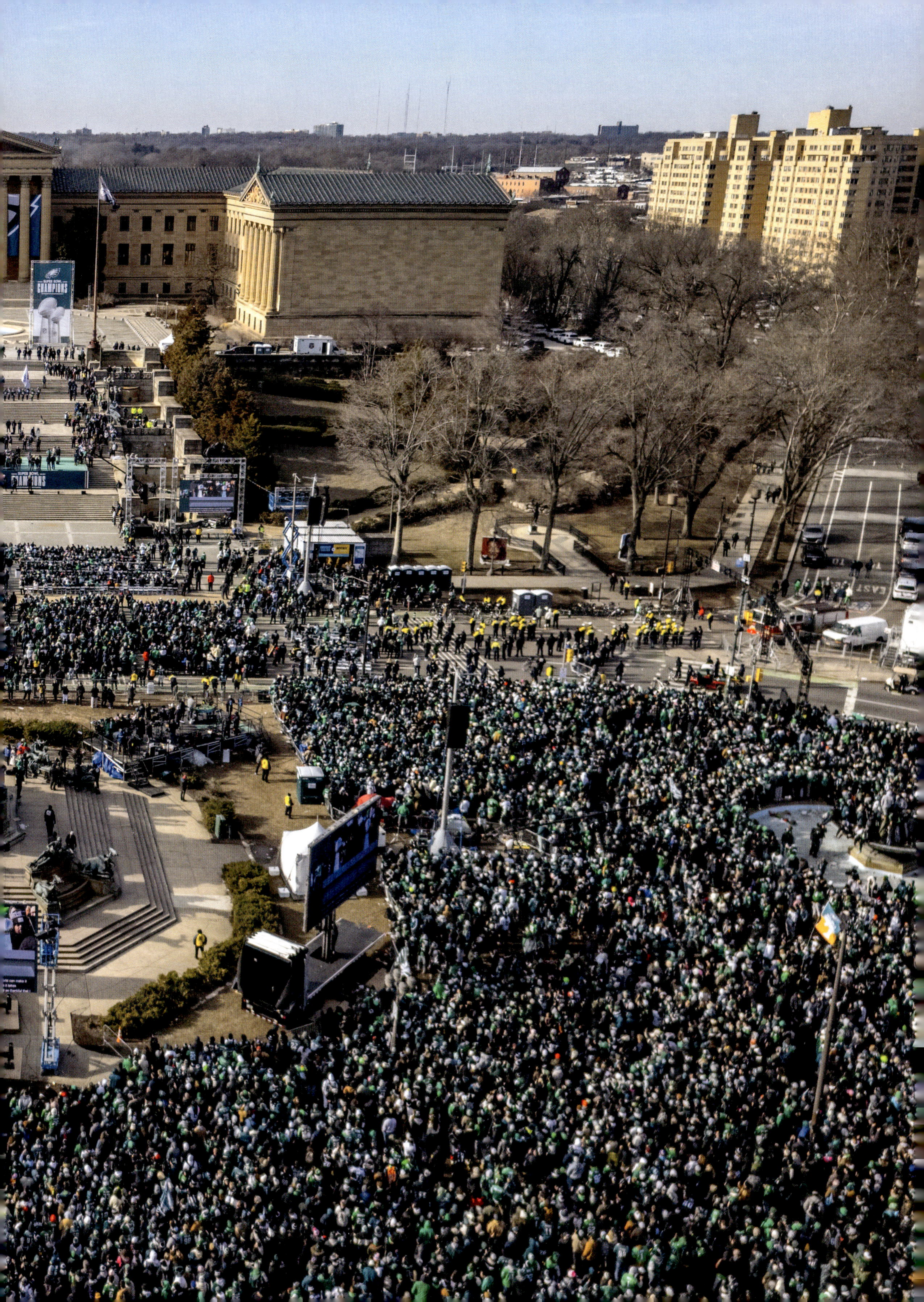
CHAMPIONS
EAST

THE PRE-GAME HYPE GETS LINCOLN FINANCIAL FIELD FIRED UP AND THE ENTIRE TEAM, FROM TOP TO BOTTOM, CONTRIBUTES TO A WORLD CHAMPIONSHIP PERFORMANCE

2024 PLAYER ROSTER

Position	No.	Player
QB	1	Jalen Hurts
	7	Kenny Pickett
	13	Ian Book
	16	Tanner McKee
RB	14	Kenneth Gainwell
	26	Saquon Barkley
	28	Will Shipley
	35	Tyrion Davis-Price
	48	Khari Blasingame
WR	6	DeVonta Smith
	11	A.J. Brown
	18	Britain Covey
	41	Danny Gray
	80	Parris Campbell
	82	Ainias Smith
	83	Jahan Dotson
	86	Kyle Philips
	89	Johnny Wilson
TE	47	C.J. Uzomah
	81	Grant Calcaterra
	84	E.J. Jenkins
	87	Nick Muse
	88	Dallas Goedert
OFFENSIVE LINE	51	Cam Jurgens
	56	Tyler Steen
	61	Nick Gates
	64	Brett Toth
	65	Lane Johnson
	67	Laekin Vakalahi
	68	Jordan Mailata
	69	Landon Dickerson
	72	Darian Kinnard
	73	Le'Raven Clark
	74	Fred Johnson
	75	Jack Driscoll
	77	Mekhi Becton
	79	Trevor Keegan
DEFENSIVE LINE	0	Bryce Huff
	50	K.J. Henry
	55	Brandon Graham
	59	Thomas Booker
	90	Jordan Davis
	93	Milton Williams
	94	Byron Young
	95	Charles Harris
	96	Gabe Hall
	97	Moro Ojomo
	98	Jalen Carter
LB	3	Nolan Smith
	17	Nakobe Dean
	19	Josh Sweat
	42	Oren Burks
	43	Nicholas Morrow
	45	Ochaun Mathis
	52	Dallas Gant
	53	Zack Baun
	54	Jeremiah Trotter Jr.
	57	Ben VanSumeren
	58	Jalyx Hunt
DEFENSIVE BACKS	2	Darius Slay
	8	C.J. Gardner-Johnson
	21	Sydney Brown
	22	Kelee Ringo
	23	Eli Ricks
	24	James Bradberry
	27	Quinyon Mitchell
	29	Avonte Maddox
	30	Parry Nickerson
	31	Andre Sam
	32	Reed Blankenship
	33	Cooper DeJean
	34	Isaiah Rodgers
	36	Tristin McCollum
	38	Lewis Cine
	39	A.J. Woods
	46	Tariq Castro-Fields
ST	4	Jake Elliott
	10	Braden Mann
	49	Rick Lovato

PHILADELPHIA EAGLES

EXECUTIVE PRODUCER
Jen Kavanagh

PROJECT DIRECTORS
Jessica Cashin
Brian Papson

COPY EDITORS
Anthony Bonagura
Ray Doyle
John Gonoude
Emily Heineman
Bob Lange
Shane Ramsey
Brett Strohsacker

WRITER
Dave Spadaro

DESIGN & CREATIVE
Christine Dorn
Donavan Edwards
Kiel Leggere

SKYBOX PRESS

EDITOR & PUBLISHER
Scott Gummer

DESIGN
SeeSullivan

PHOTOGRAPHY
Kiel Leggere, Drew Hallowell, Hunter Martin, Chrissy Obell, Brian Garfinkle, Devlynn Bunning, Nicholas Davis, Kennedy Rodriguez, Ed Mahan, and Brian Papson.

THE EAGLES WOULD LIKE TO THANK everyone involved who helped produce this look at the journey to the franchise's second world championship, including Team President Don Smolenski, Aileen Dagrosa, Tina D'Orazio, Frank Gumienny, Jen Kavanagh, Bob Lange, Jason Miller, Brian Napoli, Marla Axelrod, and Rachel Weiss.

SPECIAL THANKS TO Jewell Smolenski and Brent Lawton with the NFL.

Official publication of the National Football League

www.skyboxpress.com
info@skyboxpress.com

ISBN: 979-8-9921084-4-6

Printed in the United States of America

10 9 8 7 6 5 4 3 2 1

Published by Skybox Press, LLC.

BUD LIGHT
TOYOTA
Lincoln Financial Field
xfinity
ACME
PEPSI
BETMGM
EAGLES